Engage, Influence, Convert: Maximizing Social Media for Marketing Success

Katarina

Copyright © [2023]

Author: Katarina

Title: Engage, Influence, Convert: Maximizing Social Media for Marketing Success

This book is a product of [Publisher's Katarina]

ISBN:

TABLE OF CONTENTS

Chapter 1: Understanding Social Media's Impact on Consumer Behavior

The Rise of Social Media in Marketing

Social media has become an integral part of our lives, transforming the way we connect, communicate, and consume information. As the digital landscape continues to evolve, it is essential for businesses and marketers to recognize the power and potential of social media in reaching and engaging their target audience.

In recent years, social media platforms such as Facebook, Instagram, Twitter, and LinkedIn have experienced exponential growth. With billions of active users worldwide, these platforms have become a goldmine for marketers looking to expand their reach and drive business growth.

The impact of social media on marketing has been profound. Unlike traditional forms of advertising, social media allows businesses to engage with their audience on a more personal level. It provides a platform for direct communication, enabling brands to build relationships, gain customer insights, and establish brand loyalty.

One of the key advantages of social media marketing is its cost-effectiveness. With minimal investment, businesses can create and share content that resonates with their target audience. This democratization of marketing has leveled the playing field, allowing small businesses to compete with larger corporations and reach a global audience.

Furthermore, social media marketing offers unparalleled targeting capabilities. Platforms like Facebook and Instagram provide sophisticated algorithms that enable businesses to target specific demographics, interests, and behaviors. This precision targeting ensures that marketing efforts are directed towards the most relevant audience, maximizing the chances of conversion and ROI.

Another significant benefit of social media marketing is its ability to generate viral content. With the power of social sharing, businesses can create content that spreads like wildfire, reaching millions of users within a short span of time. This viral effect not only increases brand awareness but also enhances credibility and trust among the audience.

In conclusion, the rise of social media in marketing has revolutionized the way businesses promote their products and services. With its ability to engage, influence, and convert, social media has become an indispensable tool for marketers across all industries. By harnessing the power of social media, businesses can maximize their reach, connect with their audience on a personal level, and drive marketing success. Whether you are a seasoned marketer or just starting out, understanding and leveraging the impact of social media is crucial for staying competitive in today's digital age.

The Power of Social Media in Influencing Consumer Behavior

In today's digital age, social media has become an integral part of our daily lives. Whether it's connecting with friends and family, sharing experiences, or staying up-to-date with the latest news and trends, social media platforms have revolutionized the way we communicate and interact with the world. However, the impact of social media goes far beyond personal connections – it has also emerged as a powerful tool that can significantly influence consumer behavior.

Social media platforms have the ability to reach millions of people instantaneously, making them a prime channel for businesses to connect with their target audience. With just a few clicks, companies can share their products, services, and brand messages to a vast array of potential customers. This accessibility has transformed the marketing landscape, allowing companies of all sizes to compete on a level playing field.

One of the key factors that make social media so influential in shaping consumer behavior is the power of social proof. People tend to be influenced by the opinions and actions of others, especially those within their social circles. Social media provides an avenue for individuals to share their experiences, recommendations, and reviews, which can greatly impact the purchasing decisions of others. Whether it's a positive review from a friend or an influencer's endorsement, these social cues can create a sense of trust and credibility that traditional advertising methods struggle to achieve.

Furthermore, social media platforms offer businesses invaluable insights into their target audience. Through analytics and data tracking, companies can gain a deeper understanding of consumer preferences, behaviors, and trends. This information allows businesses to tailor their marketing strategies and offerings to better meet the needs and desires of their customers. By leveraging this knowledge, companies can create personalized and targeted content that resonates with their audience, increasing the likelihood of conversion and long-term customer loyalty.

However, it's important to note that the power of social media in influencing consumer behavior is a double-edged sword. While it can be a catalyst for positive brand exposure and growth, it can also lead to negative consequences if misused or mishandled. Negative reviews, viral controversies, and social media backlash can have detrimental effects on a company's reputation and bottom line. Therefore, it is essential for businesses to approach social media marketing with caution, ensuring that their messages are authentic, transparent, and aligned with their core values.

In conclusion, social media has become a potent force in shaping consumer behavior. Its ability to connect people, provide social proof, and offer valuable consumer insights has transformed the marketing landscape. However, businesses must tread carefully and use social media responsibly to harness its full potential. By understanding and leveraging the power of social media, companies can engage, influence, and convert their target audience, ultimately maximizing their marketing success.

The Evolution of Consumer Behavior in the Digital Age

In today's digital age, consumer behavior has undergone a significant transformation. With the advent of social media and the internet, consumers have become more empowered and connected than ever before. This subchapter explores the evolution of consumer behavior and its impact on marketing strategies in the digital era.

Gone are the days when consumers relied solely on traditional marketing channels such as television and print ads to make purchasing decisions. Today, consumers are actively seeking information, reading reviews, and engaging with brands on social media platforms. They are no longer passive recipients of marketing messages but active participants in the decision-making process.

The rise of social media has revolutionized how consumers interact with brands. They can now connect with companies directly, voice their opinions, and share their experiences with a wider audience. This has given rise to a new wave of influencer marketing, where brands leverage the power of social media influencers to reach and engage with their target audience.

Furthermore, the digital age has also given consumers access to a wealth of information at their fingertips. They can easily research products, compare prices, and read reviews before making a purchase. As a result, consumers are becoming more discerning and selective in their choices. They are no longer swayed by flashy advertisements; instead, they rely on the opinions and experiences of others to guide their decision-making process.

This shift in consumer behavior has forced marketers to adapt their strategies to meet the changing needs and expectations of their target audience. Brands now need to engage with consumers on social media platforms, provide valuable and relevant content, and actively listen and respond to their feedback. This two-way communication has become crucial in building trust and loyalty among consumers.

Moreover, the digital age has also given rise to new opportunities for personalization and customization. Marketers can now leverage data and analytics to gain insights into consumer preferences and tailor their offerings accordingly. This level of personalization not only enhances the consumer experience but also allows brands to target specific niches and increase conversion rates.

In conclusion, the evolution of consumer behavior in the digital age has had a profound impact on marketing strategies. Brands need to embrace social media and leverage its power to engage, influence, and convert their target audience. By understanding the changing needs and expectations of consumers, marketers can adapt their strategies and stay ahead in an increasingly competitive digital landscape.

Chapter 2: Leveraging Social Media for Marketing Success

Building an Effective Social Media Marketing Strategy

In today's digital age, social media has become a powerful tool for businesses to engage, influence, and convert their target audience. With millions of people actively using various social media platforms, it has become essential for companies to develop an effective social media marketing strategy to stay relevant and competitive. This subchapter will provide you with valuable insights on how to create a strong social media presence that maximizes your marketing success.

The first step in building an effective social media marketing strategy is to define your goals and objectives. Are you looking to increase brand awareness, drive website traffic, or generate leads? By identifying your specific goals, you can tailor your social media efforts to align with these objectives.

Next, it is crucial to identify your target audience. Understanding who your audience is and what platforms they use will allow you to create content that resonates with them. Conduct market research, analyze demographics, and monitor social media trends to gain insights into your audience's preferences and interests.

Once you have a clear understanding of your goals and target audience, it's time to start creating compelling content. Your content should be engaging, informative, and relevant to your audience's needs. Use visual elements such as images and videos to capture attention and make your posts stand out in the crowded social media landscape.

Consistency is key when it comes to social media marketing. Develop a content calendar and schedule your posts in advance to maintain a regular posting frequency. Interact with your audience by responding to comments, messages, and mentions promptly. Building a strong and genuine connection with your followers will enhance your brand's reputation and increase customer loyalty.

Additionally, leverage the power of social media analytics to measure the effectiveness of your strategy. Monitor key metrics such as reach, engagement, and conversions to determine what is working and what needs improvement. Adjust your strategy accordingly to optimize your results.

In conclusion, building an effective social media marketing strategy requires careful planning, audience targeting, compelling content creation, consistency, and data-driven analysis. By following these steps, you can harness the power of social media to engage, influence, and convert your target audience, ultimately maximizing your marketing success.

Identifying Target Audiences and Their Social Media Habits

In today's digital age, social media has become an integral part of our lives. It has revolutionized the way we communicate, connect, and consume information. As a result, businesses and marketers have recognized the immense potential of social media platforms for reaching their target audiences and driving marketing success. However, to effectively leverage social media for marketing purposes, it is crucial to identify your target audience and understand their social media habits.

Identifying your target audience is the first step towards creating impactful social media marketing campaigns. Every business, regardless of its niche, needs to have a clear understanding of who their ideal customers are. By pinpointing your target audience, you can tailor your content, messaging, and marketing strategies to resonate with their interests, preferences, and needs.

To identify your target audience, you can start by conducting market research. This involves collecting data, analyzing demographics, psychographics, and social media behavior to create customer personas. Customer personas are fictional representations of your ideal customers, complete with their characteristics, motivations, and social media habits. By understanding your audience's social media habits, such as the platforms they frequent, the type of content they engage with, and the times they are most active, you can optimize your marketing efforts and ensure maximum reach and engagement.

In the realm of social media impact, it is important to acknowledge that different social media platforms attract different user demographics and behaviors. For instance, while Facebook remains the most popular platform across all age groups, younger audiences tend to favor platforms like Instagram and TikTok. LinkedIn, on the other hand, caters more to professionals and businesses. By recognizing these differences, you can strategically choose the platforms that align with your target audience's social media habits and preferences.

Moreover, understanding your target audience's social media habits also enables you to create and curate content that resonates with them. By analyzing the type of content they engage with, you can identify trends, topics, and formats that are likely to capture their attention. This knowledge empowers you to craft compelling content that not only attracts but also influences and converts your target audience.

In conclusion, identifying your target audience and understanding their social media habits is imperative for maximizing social media for marketing success. By conducting thorough market research, creating customer personas, and analyzing social media behavior, you can tailor your marketing strategies to effectively engage, influence, and convert your target audience. Whether you are a business owner, marketer, or social media enthusiast, harnessing the power of social media impact begins with understanding your audience and their social media habits.

Crafting Engaging and Shareable Social Media Content

In today's digital age, social media has become a powerful tool for businesses and individuals alike to connect, engage, and influence their target audience. As social media platforms continue to evolve and grow, it is essential to understand the art of crafting engaging and shareable content that will leave a lasting impact on your audience. This subchapter aims to provide valuable insights and strategies on how to maximize the potential of your social media content to drive engagement and create a strong social media impact.

The key to creating engaging and shareable social media content lies in understanding your audience. Every successful social media campaign starts with thorough research and analysis of your target market's preferences, interests, and online behavior. By gaining a deep understanding of your audience, you can tailor your content to resonate with them effectively.

One of the first steps in crafting compelling social media content is to develop a strong content strategy. This involves setting clear goals, identifying key messages, and determining the best platforms to reach your target audience. By aligning your content strategy with your overall marketing objectives, you can ensure that your social media efforts are consistent and impactful.

To engage your audience, it is crucial to create content that is not only visually appealing but also provides value. Whether it's informative blog posts, entertaining videos, or stunning visuals, your content should be informative, entertaining, or inspiring. By consistently delivering valuable content, you can establish yourself as a trusted authority in your niche and build a loyal following.

Additionally, incorporating storytelling techniques into your social media content can significantly enhance engagement. Humans are naturally drawn to narratives, and weaving stories into your posts can evoke emotions and create a deeper connection with your audience. Sharing personal anecdotes, success stories, or customer testimonials can help humanize your brand and make it more relatable.

To maximize the shareability of your content, it is essential to optimize it for social sharing. Including attention-grabbing headlines, relevant hashtags, and visually appealing images can increase the likelihood of your content being shared by your audience. Moreover, actively encouraging social sharing by incorporating social media sharing buttons and calls-to-action can significantly amplify the reach of your content.

In conclusion, crafting engaging and shareable social media content is a critical aspect of maximizing your social media impact. By understanding your audience, developing a strong content strategy, and delivering valuable and relatable content, you can engage and influence your target market effectively. Remember, the power of social media lies in its ability to connect people, and by creating content that resonates with your audience, you can truly make a difference in your marketing success.

Chapter 3: Engaging with Social Media Users

Creating a Strong Brand Presence on Social Media

In today's digital era, social media has become an indispensable tool for individuals and businesses alike. It is not only a platform for connecting with friends, but also a powerful marketing tool to engage, influence, and convert potential customers. To maximize your social media impact, it is essential to create a strong brand presence that resonates with your target audience. This subchapter delves into effective strategies to establish a robust brand presence on social media, ensuring marketing success for everyone.

First and foremost, it is crucial to define your brand identity. What makes your brand unique? What values and beliefs do you want to convey? Understanding your brand's core essence will help you build a consistent and authentic presence across social media platforms. Consistency is key, as it reinforces your brand's image and strengthens brand recall among your audience.

Next, identify your target audience. Who are your ideal customers? Research their demographics, interests, and online behaviors to tailor your social media content accordingly. By understanding your audience, you can create engaging and relevant content that speaks directly to their needs and desires.

One effective way to establish a strong brand presence is by creating a content strategy. Plan your social media posts in advance, ensuring a mix of informative, entertaining, and promotional content. Engage your audience with captivating visuals, compelling storytelling, and interactive elements such as polls and contests. Encourage user-generated content to foster a sense of community and strengthen brand loyalty.

Consistently monitor and analyze your social media metrics to measure your brand's impact. Pay attention to engagement rates, follower growth, and audience sentiment. This data will provide valuable insights into what content resonates with your audience and how to further optimize your social media strategy.

Additionally, build relationships with influencers and brand advocates who align with your values. Collaborating with influential individuals or partnering with complementary brands can expand your reach and lend credibility to your brand.

Lastly, do not underestimate the power of customer engagement. Respond promptly to comments, messages, and reviews to demonstrate your commitment to customer satisfaction. Encourage and appreciate feedback, as it helps improve your products or services while fostering a positive brand reputation.

By creating a strong brand presence on social media, you can effectively engage, influence, and convert your target audience. Remember, social media is a dynamic and ever-evolving space, so continuously evaluate and adapt your strategies to stay ahead of the curve. Embrace the potential of social media marketing, and watch your brand thrive in the digital realm!

Building Authentic Connections with Social Media Users

In today's digital age, social media has become an integral part of our lives. It has transformed the way we connect, communicate, and share information. With billions of users across various platforms, social media has immense potential to impact individuals and businesses alike. However, to truly harness the power of social media, it is essential to build authentic connections with users.

Authenticity is the cornerstone of successful social media marketing. Users are increasingly seeking genuine interactions and relationships, making it crucial for businesses to establish trust and credibility. Building authentic connections not only helps businesses engage with their target audience but also enables them to influence and convert potential customers.

To build authentic connections, businesses need to understand their audience's needs, interests, and preferences. This involves conducting thorough research and analysis to identify the demographics, psychographics, and behaviors of their target market. By gaining insights into their audience's motivations and desires, businesses can tailor their content and messaging to resonate with them on a deeper level.

Another key aspect of building authentic connections is active engagement. Social media platforms offer numerous opportunities for businesses to interact with their audience. Responding to comments, messages, and reviews in a timely and personalized manner demonstrates that businesses genuinely care about their customers. By actively engaging with users, businesses can foster a sense of community and loyalty, making their audience more receptive to their marketing efforts.

Authenticity can also be established by sharing behind-the-scenes content and showcasing the human side of the business. By giving users a glimpse into the people, processes, and stories behind the brand, businesses can create a more relatable and trustworthy image. This can be done through live videos, employee spotlights, customer testimonials, and other forms of user-generated content. Such content not only humanizes the brand but also encourages users to engage and share their own experiences.

In conclusion, building authentic connections with social media users is paramount for businesses aiming to maximize their marketing success. By understanding their audience, actively engaging with users, and showcasing the human side of the brand, businesses can establish trust, credibility, and loyalty. In doing so, they create a community of loyal followers who are not only influenced by their marketing efforts but also become advocates for their brand.

Encouraging User Engagement and Participation

In today's digital era, social media has become an integral part of our lives. It has transformed the way we communicate, interact, and share information with others. With billions of people actively using various social media platforms, businesses are presented with an incredible opportunity to engage and influence their target audience. This subchapter will delve into the importance of user engagement and participation in social media, and how it can significantly impact your marketing success.

User engagement refers to the level of involvement, interaction, and interest users show towards your social media content. It is not merely about the number of followers or likes but about creating meaningful connections with your audience. To achieve this, it is essential to provide valuable, relevant, and entertaining content that resonates with your target demographic. By delivering content that addresses their needs, challenges, and interests, you can foster a sense of community and encourage active participation.

One effective way to encourage user engagement is by asking questions or conducting polls that invite your audience to share their opinions or experiences. This not only makes users feel valued and heard but also offers insights into their preferences and behaviors. Additionally, responding promptly to comments, messages, and mentions will make your audience feel acknowledged and appreciated, further boosting engagement levels.

Another crucial aspect of encouraging user engagement is to create a two-way dialogue. Instead of solely broadcasting information, actively seek out and respond to user-generated content, such as comments, reviews, and shares. By acknowledging and showcasing user-generated content, you not only demonstrate your appreciation but also build trust and credibility among your audience.

Furthermore, hosting contests, giveaways, or challenges can significantly boost user participation. These interactive activities not only capture attention but also incentivize users to engage with your brand. By incorporating a call-to-action, such as sharing, tagging friends, or creating user-generated content, you can amplify your reach and visibility across social media platforms.

Lastly, regularly monitoring and analyzing social media metrics is crucial to understand what content resonates the most with your audience. By tracking engagement rates, click-through rates, and other relevant metrics, you can identify patterns and make informed decisions about the type of content and strategies that yield the highest user engagement.

In conclusion, user engagement and participation are vital for maximizing social media marketing success. By creating valuable content, fostering a sense of community, and actively engaging with your audience, you can create a loyal following, build brand awareness, and drive meaningful conversions. Remember, social media is not just a platform for broadcasting; it is an opportunity to authentically connect with your audience and create a lasting impact.

Chapter 4: Influencing Consumer Behavior through Social Media

Harnessing the Power of Social Media Influencers

In today's digital age, social media has become an integral part of our lives. It has revolutionized the way we interact, communicate, and even make purchasing decisions. As a result, businesses and marketers are constantly seeking innovative ways to tap into the immense potential of social media platforms. One such strategy that has gained significant traction is harnessing the power of social media influencers.

Social media influencers are individuals who have built a substantial following on various platforms such as Instagram, YouTube, or TikTok. They have the ability to impact their audience's opinions, behavior, and purchasing decisions through their authentic content and engagement. Leveraging their reach and influence can be a game-changer for businesses looking to maximize their social media marketing success.

The first step in harnessing the power of social media influencers is identifying the right ones for your niche. Conduct thorough research to find influencers whose audience aligns with your target market. Look for individuals who have a genuine interest in your industry and whose values align with your brand. Collaborating with influencers who are passionate about your product or service will ensure their recommendations are authentic and resonate with their followers.

Once you have identified potential influencers, it is crucial to establish a strong relationship with them. Reach out to them and propose a mutually beneficial partnership. Offer incentives such as free products, exclusive discounts, or even financial compensation for their endorsements. Building a solid relationship with influencers can result in long-term partnerships, allowing for continuous exposure to their audience.

When working with influencers, it is essential to give them creative freedom. Influencers have a unique understanding of their audience, and they know what content will resonate best. Allowing them to create content that aligns with their style and tone will result in more authentic and engaging posts. Encourage them to share their personal experiences and genuine opinions about your product or service, as this will foster trust and credibility among their followers.

In conclusion, harnessing the power of social media influencers can significantly impact your marketing success. By identifying the right influencers, building strong relationships, and giving them creative freedom, you can tap into their extensive reach and influence. Remember, authenticity is key. Collaborating with influencers who genuinely believe in your brand will yield the most effective results. So, embrace the power of social media influencers and watch your business thrive in the digital realm.

Utilizing User-Generated Content to Drive Conversions

In today's digital age, social media has become an integral part of our daily lives, influencing how we communicate, connect, and make purchasing decisions. As businesses strive to maximize their marketing success, it is crucial to leverage the power of user-generated content (UGC) to drive conversions. UGC refers to any content created and shared by users, such as reviews, testimonials, photos, videos, or social media posts. This subchapter explores the impact of UGC on social media and how businesses can harness its potential to boost their conversion rates.

UGC holds immense power in influencing consumer behavior. When potential customers see authentic and relatable content created by fellow users, they are more likely to trust and engage with a brand. Research shows that UGC has a significant impact on purchase decisions, with 79% of consumers stating that UGC highly influences their purchasing choices. By incorporating UGC into their marketing strategies, businesses can effectively engage and influence their target audience, ultimately driving conversions.

One of the primary benefits of UGC is its ability to foster brand advocacy. When customers share their positive experiences with a brand through UGC, they are essentially becoming brand ambassadors, spreading the word and generating buzz. By encouraging and incentivizing customers to create and share UGC, businesses can tap into this powerful form of social proof and leverage it to boost their credibility and conversions.

To effectively utilize UGC, businesses need to create an environment that encourages content creation. This can be achieved by running contests, offering rewards or discounts for UGC, or simply asking customers to share their experiences. By actively engaging with their audience and showcasing UGC on their social media platforms or websites, businesses can create a sense of community and authenticity. Moreover, by curating and repurposing UGC, companies can extend the lifespan of this content and maximize its impact.

Monitoring and analyzing the performance of UGC is crucial for measuring its effectiveness and optimizing conversion rates. By tracking engagement metrics, sentiment analysis, and conversion data, businesses can gain insights into what type of UGC resonates best with their audience and make data-driven decisions to enhance their marketing strategies.

In conclusion, user-generated content has a profound impact on social media and can be a potent tool for driving conversions. By leveraging UGC, businesses can tap into the power of social proof, foster brand advocacy, and create a sense of authenticity that resonates with their audience. By actively encouraging and curating UGC, and by analyzing its performance, businesses can maximize their social media impact and achieve marketing success.

Leveraging Social Proof and Social Media Recommendations

In today's digital age, social media has become an integral part of our lives. From connecting with friends and family to discovering new products and services, social media platforms have revolutionized the way we interact and make purchase decisions. As a result, businesses and marketers have recognized the immense potential of leveraging social proof and social media recommendations to drive marketing success.

Social proof refers to the phenomenon where individuals look to others for guidance on how to behave or make decisions. It is a powerful psychological principle that can significantly influence consumer behavior. When people see others endorsing a particular product or service on social media, they are more likely to trust and consider it for themselves. This is where social media recommendations play a crucial role.

Social media recommendations are essentially endorsements or testimonials shared by individuals on various social media platforms. These recommendations can take the form of reviews, ratings, comments, or even influencers endorsing a product or service. When people see positive recommendations from others, they develop a sense of trust and credibility towards the brand, increasing the likelihood of engagement and conversion.

For businesses and marketers, leveraging social proof and social media recommendations can yield incredible results. By strategically incorporating user-generated content, testimonials, and influencer partnerships into their social media marketing strategies, they can amplify their brand's reach and impact. Here are a few ways to maximize the benefits of social proof and social media recommendations:

1. Encourage User-Generated Content: Actively encourage your customers to share their experiences and opinions about your brand on social media. Run contests, offer incentives, or simply ask for feedback to generate authentic user-generated content that can serve as powerful social proof.

2. Collaborate with Influencers: Identify influencers in your niche who have a strong following and align with your brand values. Partnering with them to promote your products or services can significantly enhance your credibility and expand your reach to their loyal followers.

3. Monitor and Respond to Reviews: Stay vigilant about monitoring online reviews and comments about your brand. Address any negative feedback promptly and professionally, demonstrating your commitment to customer satisfaction. Positive responses can further reinforce the social proof provided by satisfied customers.

4. Leverage Social Media Listening Tools: Utilize social media listening tools to track mentions and conversations related to your brand. This valuable data can help you identify trends, sentiments, and opportunities for engaging with your audience in real-time.

In conclusion, leveraging social proof and social media recommendations is crucial for businesses and marketers looking to maximize their social media impact. By harnessing the power of user-generated content, influencer partnerships, and online reviews, they can build trust, credibility, and ultimately, drive conversions. So, start implementing these strategies and watch your brand's social media presence soar to new heights.

Chapter 5: Converting Social Media Engagement into Sales

Implementing Effective Social Media Advertising Strategies

In today's digital age, social media has become an integral part of our lives. It has revolutionized the way people connect, communicate, and share information. As a result, businesses have recognized the immense potential of social media as a marketing tool. However, merely having a presence on social media is not enough to achieve marketing success. To truly engage, influence, and convert your target audience, it is crucial to implement effective social media advertising strategies.

One of the first steps to developing an effective social media advertising strategy is to clearly define your goals. Are you looking to increase brand awareness, drive website traffic, or generate leads? Understanding your objectives will help you tailor your advertising efforts accordingly.

Identifying your target audience is another essential component of effective social media advertising. By knowing who your audience is, you can create content that resonates with them and delivers value. Conduct thorough research to understand their demographics, interests, and online behaviors, and use this information to craft personalized advertisements that capture their attention.

Once you have identified your target audience, it is important to select the right social media platforms for your advertising campaigns. Each platform has its unique strengths and demographics, so choose the platforms that align with your target audience and marketing goals. Whether it's Facebook, Instagram, Twitter, or LinkedIn, tailor your content to suit the platform and engage with your audience effectively.

To maximize the impact of your social media advertising, it is essential to create compelling and visually appealing content. Utilize high-quality images, videos, and infographics that grab the audience's attention and convey your messaging effectively. Craft compelling ad copies that are concise, engaging, and persuasive, encouraging users to take action.

Monitoring and analyzing the performance of your social media advertising campaigns is crucial for ongoing success. Utilize analytics tools provided by the social media platforms to track key metrics such as reach, engagement, and conversions. Use this data to refine your strategies, optimize your campaigns, and make data-driven decisions to improve your return on investment.

In conclusion, implementing effective social media advertising strategies is essential to maximize your social media impact. By clearly defining your goals, understanding your target audience, selecting the right platforms, creating compelling content, and analyzing performance, you can engage, influence, and convert your audience successfully. Stay up to date with emerging trends and continuously refine your strategies to stay ahead in the ever-evolving world of social media marketing.

Optimizing Social Media Platforms for Lead Generation

In today's fast-paced digital world, social media has become an integral part of our lives. From connecting with friends and family to sharing personal experiences, social media platforms have evolved into powerful marketing tools for businesses. If utilized effectively, they can significantly impact a company's lead generation efforts.

In this subchapter, we will explore strategies and techniques for optimizing social media platforms to generate leads. Whether you are a small business owner, an entrepreneur, or a marketing professional, understanding the potential of social media for lead generation is crucial to your success in today's competitive market.

Firstly, it is important to identify the social media platforms that align with your target audience and business goals. Each platform caters to different demographics and user behaviors. For instance, Facebook is known for its diverse user base, while Instagram appeals to a younger demographic with a focus on visual content. By understanding your audience's preferences, you can tailor your content and engagement strategies accordingly.

Once you have selected the appropriate platforms, the next step is to create compelling and engaging content. High-quality and relevant content not only attracts attention but also establishes your brand as an industry leader. Consider utilizing a mix of formats, such as videos, infographics, and blog posts, to cater to different user preferences. Remember to incorporate strong call-to-actions (CTAs) in your content to encourage users to take the desired action, such as signing up for a newsletter or downloading an ebook.

Additionally, social media platforms offer various lead generation tools that can amplify your efforts. For example, Facebook Ads and Instagram Ads allow you to target specific audiences based on demographics, interests, and behaviors. By leveraging these tools, you can reach a wider audience and increase your chances of generating quality leads.

Another effective strategy is to actively engage with your audience. Respond to comments, messages, and reviews promptly to build trust and foster relationships. Encourage user-generated content and testimonials to enhance your brand's credibility. By creating a sense of community and actively interacting with your followers, you will increase the likelihood of converting them into valuable leads.

In conclusion, social media platforms have immense potential when it comes to lead generation. By optimizing your strategies, creating compelling content, utilizing lead generation tools, and actively engaging with your audience, you can maximize the impact of social media on your marketing success. Remember, social media is not just about gaining followers; it's about converting those followers into loyal customers.

Tracking and Analyzing Social Media Metrics for Conversion

In today's digital age, social media has become an integral part of our lives. It has transformed the way we communicate, connect, and even shop. For businesses, harnessing the power of social media is no longer optional but a necessity. However, merely having a presence on social media platforms is not enough. To truly maximize social media for marketing success, it is crucial to track and analyze social media metrics for conversion.

Tracking social media metrics allows businesses to measure the effectiveness of their social media efforts and understand the impact they are making on their target audience. By analyzing the metrics, businesses can gain valuable insights into what is working and what needs improvement. This enables them to make data-driven decisions and optimize their social media strategies to drive conversions.

There are several key social media metrics that businesses should track and analyze. One of the most important metrics is reach, which indicates how many people have seen a particular social media post or campaign. This metric helps businesses understand the visibility and potential reach of their content. Another crucial metric is engagement, which measures how users are interacting with the content, such as likes, comments, and shares. High engagement signifies that the content is resonating with the audience and generating interest.

Furthermore, tracking click-through rates (CTRs) is essential to measure the effectiveness of social media campaigns in driving traffic to the business website. This metric provides insights into the quality of the content and its ability to capture the audience's attention and interest. Additionally, conversion metrics, such as lead generation and sales, are vital in determining the return on investment (ROI) of social media marketing efforts.

To effectively track and analyze social media metrics for conversion, businesses can utilize various tools and platforms specifically designed for this purpose. These tools provide comprehensive analytics, allowing businesses to monitor their social media performance, identify trends, and make informed decisions. Moreover, businesses should establish clear goals and objectives and align their social media metrics with these goals to measure success accurately.

In conclusion, tracking and analyzing social media metrics for conversion is crucial for businesses looking to maximize their social media impact. By understanding the effectiveness of their social media efforts, businesses can optimize their strategies, enhance engagement, and drive conversions. With the availability of various tracking tools and platforms, businesses can harness the power of data to make informed decisions and achieve marketing success in the social media landscape.

Chapter 6: Maximizing Social Media ROI

Integrating Social Media with Other Marketing Channels

In today's digital age, social media has emerged as a powerful tool for businesses to engage with their target audience, influence their purchasing decisions, and ultimately convert them into loyal customers. However, to fully maximize the potential of social media for marketing success, it is crucial to integrate it with other marketing channels.

Effective integration of social media with other marketing channels can enhance brand visibility, extend reach, and drive more meaningful customer interactions. By combining social media with traditional marketing channels such as print, television, or radio, businesses can create a cohesive and comprehensive marketing strategy that resonates with their target audience across various touchpoints.

One of the key advantages of integrating social media with other marketing channels is the ability to amplify messaging. By leveraging the power of social media platforms, businesses can extend the reach of their marketing campaigns and increase brand exposure. For example, a television advertisement can be promoted on social media platforms, allowing viewers to engage with the brand and share their experiences with their social networks, thereby increasing the campaign's impact.

Additionally, integrating social media with other marketing channels can provide valuable insights and data. By monitoring social media conversations and engagement metrics, businesses can gain real-time feedback about their marketing efforts. This feedback can be used to fine-tune marketing strategies and create more personalized and relevant content for the target audience.

Furthermore, integrating social media with other marketing channels enables businesses to create a seamless customer experience. By leveraging social media platforms as customer service channels, businesses can provide timely responses to customer inquiries, address concerns, and build stronger relationships. This integration also allows businesses to redirect customers from social media platforms to other marketing channels such as websites, blogs, or email campaigns, providing a holistic brand experience.

In conclusion, integrating social media with other marketing channels is essential for businesses looking to maximize the impact of their social media strategies. By combining social media with traditional marketing channels, businesses can amplify messaging, gain valuable insights, and create a seamless customer experience. Regardless of your industry or niche, integrating social media with other marketing channels is a must to engage, influence, and convert your target audience successfully.

Scaling and Automating Social Media Marketing Efforts

In today's digital age, social media has become an integral part of our lives. It has transformed the way people communicate, share information, and make purchasing decisions. For businesses, harnessing the power of social media is crucial to stay relevant and competitive in the market. However, managing social media marketing efforts can be time-consuming and overwhelming, especially as your business grows. This is where scaling and automating social media marketing efforts come into play.

Scaling your social media marketing efforts involves expanding your reach and impact across various platforms. It is essential to identify the social media platforms that are most relevant to your target audience and focus your efforts on those channels. By doing so, you can optimize your resources and ensure that your message reaches the right people.

Automation tools play a vital role in scaling social media marketing efforts. These tools help streamline and automate repetitive tasks, such as scheduling posts, monitoring engagement, and analyzing metrics. By automating these processes, you can save time and effort, allowing you to focus on creating engaging content and building relationships with your audience.

One of the key benefits of automation is the ability to schedule posts in advance. This feature enables you to maintain a consistent presence on social media, even when you're not available to manually post updates. By planning and scheduling your content in advance, you can ensure that your audience receives regular updates and stays engaged with your brand.

Another aspect of scaling and automating social media marketing efforts is leveraging data and analytics. By tracking metrics such as reach, engagement, and conversions, you can gain valuable insights into what is working and what needs improvement. This data-driven approach allows you to refine your social media strategy and optimize your marketing efforts for better results.

However, while automation can be a powerful tool, it's crucial to strike a balance between automation and personalization. Social media is all about building relationships and connecting with your audience. Therefore, it's essential to maintain a human touch and engage with your followers on a personal level. Remember to respond to comments and messages promptly and authentically to foster a sense of community and trust.

In conclusion, scaling and automating social media marketing efforts are vital for businesses to maximize their social media impact. By leveraging automation tools and data-driven insights, you can streamline your processes, save time, and optimize your marketing efforts. However, it's essential to maintain a balance between automation and personalization to build meaningful connections with your audience. By mastering the art of scaling and automating social media marketing, you can engage, influence, and convert your audience effectively, driving marketing success for your brand.

Measuring and Improving Social Media Marketing Success

In today's digital age, social media has become an integral part of our lives. From connecting with friends and family to discovering new products and services, it has revolutionized the way we communicate and do business. As a result, understanding and harnessing the power of social media marketing has become crucial for individuals and businesses alike.

Measuring the success of your social media marketing efforts is essential to ensure that you are on the right track and making the most of your resources. This subchapter will delve into the key metrics and tools that can help you evaluate the impact of your social media campaigns.

First and foremost, it is important to identify the goals of your social media marketing strategy. Are you aiming to increase brand awareness, drive website traffic, generate leads, or boost sales? Each objective requires a different set of metrics to measure success. For instance, brand awareness can be evaluated through reach, impressions, and engagement, while lead generation can be measured by the number of conversions and click-through rates.

Once your goals are defined, you can utilize various analytics tools to track and monitor your social media performance. Platforms such as Facebook Insights, Twitter Analytics, and Google Analytics provide valuable insights into audience demographics, engagement rates, and referral traffic. These tools enable you to identify which social media channels are driving the most traffic and conversions, allowing you to focus your efforts and resources accordingly.

Improving social media marketing success is an ongoing process that requires continuous monitoring, analysis, and adaptation. It is crucial to regularly review your social media metrics to identify trends and patterns. By understanding what content resonates with your audience, you can refine your strategy and create more engaging and impactful posts.

Additionally, engaging with your audience is vital for social media success. Responding to comments, messages, and reviews demonstrates your commitment to customer satisfaction and builds trust. Monitoring social media sentiment can help you identify areas of improvement and address any negative feedback promptly.

In conclusion, measuring and improving social media marketing success is essential in today's digital landscape. By setting clear objectives, utilizing analytics tools, and continuously adapting your strategy, you can maximize the impact of your social media efforts. Remember, social media is a dynamic and ever-evolving platform, so staying informed and agile is key to achieving marketing success in this space.

Chapter 7: Future Trends in Social Media Marketing

Emerging Technologies and Their Impact on Social Media

In today's fast-paced digital world, social media has become an integral part of our lives. It has revolutionized the way we communicate, share information, and connect with others. However, the landscape of social media is constantly evolving, with new technologies emerging that are shaping the way we interact and engage online. This subchapter explores the impact of these emerging technologies on social media and delves into the potential they hold for marketers and individuals alike.

One of the most significant emerging technologies in recent years is artificial intelligence (AI). AI-powered algorithms have transformed the way content is curated and distributed on social media platforms. These algorithms analyze user behavior, preferences, and interests to deliver personalized content, making social media platforms more engaging and relevant. Marketers can leverage AI to tailor their messaging and advertisements, ensuring they reach the right audience at the right time. Additionally, chatbots powered by AI are enhancing customer service experiences by providing instant responses and support, further enhancing brand-consumer interactions.

Another emerging technology with a profound impact on social media is augmented reality (AR). AR allows users to overlay digital elements onto the real world, creating immersive and interactive experiences. Social media platforms like Snapchat and Instagram have integrated AR filters and effects, allowing users to transform their photos and videos with virtual objects. Brands can leverage AR to create unique and engaging content, enabling users to try products virtually or experience branded events through their smartphones. This technology presents tremendous opportunities for marketers to create memorable and shareable experiences that resonate with their target audience.

Blockchain technology is yet another emerging trend that is disrupting social media. With its decentralized and transparent nature, blockchain can address issues of trust, security, and privacy on social media platforms. Users can have more control over their data and verify the authenticity of content. Blockchain-based social media platforms are emerging, allowing users to earn rewards for their contributions and ensuring fair monetization of content. This technology has the potential to revolutionize how individuals engage with social media and how marketers target and reward their audience.

As these emerging technologies continue to evolve, it is crucial for marketers and individuals to stay informed and adapt to the changing social media landscape. By embracing these technologies, marketers can enhance their strategies, reach a wider audience, and create more meaningful connections. Individuals can benefit from a more personalized and immersive social media experience, where their preferences and interests are at the forefront. The impact of emerging technologies on social media is vast, and it is an exciting time to explore the possibilities they bring to the table.

In conclusion, the emergence of technologies such as AI, AR, and blockchain is reshaping social media as we know it. The impact of these technologies is far-reaching, offering marketers new ways to engage their audience and individuals a more personalized social media experience. By embracing these technologies, we can unlock the full potential of social media and harness its power for marketing success and personal growth.

The Role of Artificial Intelligence in Social Media Marketing

In today's digital age, social media has become an integral part of our lives. It has transformed the way we connect, communicate, and consume information. With billions of active users on various platforms, social media has also become a goldmine for marketers looking to engage with their target audience. However, the sheer volume of data and the rapidly changing nature of social media can be overwhelming. This is where artificial intelligence (AI) comes into play.

AI refers to the simulation of human intelligence in machines that are programmed to think, learn, and problem-solve like humans. When applied to social media marketing, AI can have a profound impact on a brand's success. AI algorithms can analyze vast amounts of data, identify patterns, and provide valuable insights into consumer behavior. This allows marketers to make data-driven decisions, refine their strategies, and personalize their content to resonate with their target audience.

One of the key roles of AI in social media marketing is automating repetitive tasks. AI-powered chatbots, for instance, can instantly respond to customer inquiries, offer personalized recommendations, and even facilitate transactions. This not only streamlines customer service but also frees up valuable time for marketers to focus on more strategic initiatives.

AI algorithms can also analyze social media conversations in real-time, enabling marketers to monitor sentiments, identify emerging trends, and respond promptly to customer feedback. This proactive approach helps build brand loyalty and creates a positive brand image.

Furthermore, AI can enhance social media advertising by optimizing targeting and ad placement. By analyzing user behavior, interests, and demographics, AI algorithms can deliver highly personalized ads to the right audience at the right time. This increases the effectiveness of ad campaigns, improves ROI, and reduces wasted ad spend.

In addition, AI can help marketers curate and create engaging content. By analyzing user preferences, AI algorithms can recommend relevant content to users, increasing their engagement and time spent on social media platforms. AI-powered tools can also generate content ideas, identify trending topics, and even create compelling visuals and videos.

However, it is important to note that while AI can automate and optimize social media marketing, a human touch is still crucial. AI should be seen as a tool to augment human capabilities, rather than replace them entirely. Marketers should leverage AI to gather insights, automate mundane tasks, and enhance their strategies, while still maintaining a human connection with their audience.

In conclusion, the role of artificial intelligence in social media marketing cannot be underestimated. It empowers marketers to make data-driven decisions, automate repetitive tasks, optimize ad campaigns, and create engaging content. As social media continues to evolve, AI will play an increasingly vital role in helping brands engage, influence, and convert their audience for marketing success.

Predicting and Adapting to Changing Consumer Behavior on Social Media

In today's digital age, social media has become an integral part of our daily lives. It has not only transformed the way we connect with friends and family but has also revolutionized the way businesses market their products and services. As social media continues to evolve, it is crucial for marketers to stay ahead of the curve by predicting and adapting to changing consumer behavior.

Consumer behavior on social media is constantly changing, driven by various factors such as technological advancements, cultural shifts, and emerging trends. To effectively engage and influence consumers, marketers need to understand these changes and adapt their strategies accordingly.

One of the key aspects of predicting consumer behavior on social media is analyzing data and trends. By tracking social media metrics, marketers can gain insights into the preferences, interests, and behaviors of their target audience. This data can help identify emerging trends and consumer patterns, allowing marketers to tailor their content and messaging to align with consumer expectations.

Another important factor to consider is the impact of influencers on consumer behavior. Influencer marketing has gained significant traction in recent years, with consumers often relying on recommendations and endorsements from trusted influencers. Marketers need to identify relevant influencers within their niche and establish partnerships to amplify their brand message and engage with their target audience.

Moreover, marketers must be proactive in monitoring and responding to consumer feedback on social media. Social listening tools can help identify consumer sentiment, allowing marketers to address concerns, resolve issues, and improve their overall customer experience. By actively engaging with consumers on social media, businesses can build trust and loyalty, ultimately converting followers into customers.

Additionally, marketers should keep an eye on emerging social media platforms and trends. As new platforms and features are introduced, consumer behavior can shift accordingly. By staying abreast of these developments, marketers can identify opportunities to reach their target audience in new and innovative ways.

In conclusion, predicting and adapting to changing consumer behavior on social media is crucial for marketing success. By analyzing data, leveraging influencers, actively engaging with consumers, and staying updated on emerging trends, marketers can effectively engage, influence, and convert their target audience. With social media continuing to evolve, it is essential for marketers to stay vigilant and agile in order to maximize the impact of their social media efforts.